YOUR PAIN
is your
GLORY

YOUR PAIN
is your
GLORY

Singlehood to Marital Bliss

YVONNE KUBI

XULON PRESS

Xulon Press
2301 Lucien Way #415
Maitland, FL 32751
407.339.4217
www.xulonpress.com

Due to the changing nature of the Internet, if there are any web addresses, links, or URLs included in this manuscript, these may have been altered and may no longer be accessible. The views and opinions shared in this book belong solely to the author and do not necessarily reflect those of the publisher. The publisher therefore disclaims responsibility for the views or opinions expressed within the work.

Unless otherwise indicated, Scripture quotations taken from The Message (MSG). Copyright © 1993, 1994, 1995, 1996, 2000, 2001, 2002. Used by permission of NavPress Publishing Group. Used by permission. All rights reserved.

Paperback ISBN-13: 978-1-66283-156-0

DEDICATION

This book is dedicated to my children and those who inspired me to greatness, especially the Almighty God, who oversees my life. Thank you for believing in me.

Proverbs 19:21

There are many plans in a man's heart, nevertheless the Lord's counsel that will stand.

TABLE OF CONTENTS

INTRODUCTION:

B eing Single is a blessing in disguise, and marriage is
a lifetime decision. You can waste away your youth
if you do not understand your purpose of being single,
and you can rush into marriage not knowing the details
of staying in that marriage. Love is not a gooey or mushy
feeling, but it is the ability to give sacrificially when the
other person does not even deserve it. With that said,
kindly change your mindset. Your pain can also be a con-
duit for God's glory during this crucial process. The thou-
sands of marriages that end up in divorce can be salvaged
if only we make the right decisions. Choose wisely and
change your mindset today.

CHAPTER
1

GODLY PASSION

Without the presence of God, personally, I do not know how I would strive in life. It is particularly important to live, breathe and walk with God. Without HIM, nothing can be completed. A daily walk with God will do you good.

God is a creator, so He wants you to create as a single or married person. He created you for a purpose, and His will for your life must happen. Everything you need is in the word of God, and if you seek after Him, you will find your worth and His will for your life.

Young ladies and young men, your decision to stay single or to get married is not something that just came up. God is sitting high and looking low. He knows exactly what you need, but the only way to know His will for your life is for you to seek after Him.

How do you seek after him? First, you must understand that you are a spiritual being, and with that said, you must accept Jesus as your personal savior. Secondly, find a good church to go to and depend on and trust in Him daily.

Societal pressure or desperation to get into marriage is a mistake waiting to happen. This is a crucial time for you not to make careless mistakes while single. Your greatest joy is to find someone that you can live with for the rest of your life. Being happily married is a choice. A purposed, prepared, God-fearing and mature woman or a man will bring joy and meaning to a God-ordained marriage. The time of singlehood is an exciting time to be exceptionally magnetic.

Not making the right decision in marriage will cost you. Think about your peace, children, goals, and your sanity. It will be better to stay single than to make this terrible mistake. Marriage is a covenant, and we should treat it as such. Marriage can be enjoyable and peaceful only if you meet the right person in the process. The savior of our soul can lead and direct you to this chosen individual if only you diligently walk with God. Choose wisely!

The presence of God is powerful, and the mysteries of God can be unfolding to you while single or married. The presence of God gives you the stamina to endure every life challenges. His presence brings about illumination and success. It is a gift to gain wisdom and understanding from the creator of the universe. Wisdom is God, and with understanding, He will unfold His plan to you.

Sometimes wisdom speaks at the quietness of the midnight hour and sometimes during the valley experiences. The valley experiences are contributing factors of your glory in the making. Without painful experiences, you are doomed to fail at your rising.

Some rise to excellent positions in life, and we are glad for them, but your character, charisma, enthusiasm, patience, and endurance will keep you in that position permanently. When you are passionate enough to go to His presence, self-gratification and self-praise will soon disappear because you are not working on your timetable but for Him and mankind.

Your passion is to change lives wherever you are, one day at a time. Being single or married is to glorify God.

This is a time for you to arise and learn from others while you can. Prepare yourself and do God's bidding. What you are and what you will become is in His presence. Do not forget about that. You are nothing without the stamp of the Great I Am.

God can use any platform to speak to you during this important decision-making process. Do not take this process lightly. The Holy Spirit can talk to you in diverse ways. Take heed of His promptings and guidance. Being nonchalant and careless can cost you a great deal. The Holy Spirit can use dreams and other means to connect you to your soul mate. Stay connected to your God!

CHAPTER
2

YOUR SERVICES
TO THE WORLD

Our purpose here on this earth is to serve each other. No matter how rich or how poor you are, you must end up serving somebody. My fellow brothers and sisters, do not be high-minded. The wise God has a purpose and a plan for you being in the state you are.

In the book of Ruth, Ruth did serve in Boaz's field and was not looking for fame or looking for financial help. She was looking for a relationship, but she served first. Just imagine her being a Moabite; she went through some challenges, but she was calm, cool, and collected while widowed. When Boaz met Ruth, he was already established.

God will set you up with the right person in Jesus' name. It is important you prepare yourself.

Esther was preparing herself for the King. The King knew his purpose and was looking for a woman who could be reliable, submissive, and hardworking. She used her beauty to save a nation. Vashti, the King's wife was stubborn, rude, controlling and not suitable to stay in her marriage. Preparation during singlehood is necessary!

Jacob worked hard in Laban's household so he could win the heart of Rachael. His first choice was not Laban's first daughter, Leah, but he did everything in his power to win the heart of Rachael. He loved Racheal. Jacob did not really love Leah. It will be sad to get married to someone who does not have a purpose in life. True love should be genuine.

Your service to the world is connected to your skills and talents. During singlehood, serve in the church and keep yourself busy in the things of God. Learn how to cook. Clean and groom yourself for that queen or King. You will be happy you did!

The assignment that is set before you is for the Lord to reveal unto you. Your gifts and talents will bring you before great people. For example, until you go through the valley experience, you can never experience what God has already placed in you.

Joseph was thrown into a dungeon and sold into slavery, but he never forgot about his talents. That is the reason your enemies can do their best to hurt you, but they can never touch the God-given skills that God has given to you. Joseph was in prison but was an awesome administrator and a leader. A thousand years is like a day for God. Favor is divine help, and divine assistance. Favor is God in partnership with men, providing assistance to your destiny.

Joseph had favor with God and with men. We all need favor to achieve our goals and to lead out to our destiny. Eventually, Joseph had favor with the King and helped many in his generation. His services to Potiphar were needed and valued. Joseph was exceptionally valuable because he provided solutions that were useful to society. Never think that you have arrived! Keep learning, keep striving, keep pushing and keep investing in yourself.

Whatever you find yourself doing, do it with your whole heart because you never know where God is taking you next. Ladies and Gentlemen, you may be chosen to deliver your family from ancestral curses and the issues of life. God will begin to lead and guide you into your goals.

You are called to influence people for His kingdom because of His calling on your life. You will need the supernatural wisdom of God to proceed in this dimension. Search for wisdom because the lack of wisdom is costly. There is some dimension of wisdom that comes through pain. You can ask brother Job in the bible. After Job's pain, he possessed more than he bargained for. The proof of passion is pursuit. Ignorance in this lifetime is costly. God, please give us an encounter of this wisdom so we can be of service to you and men.

> In Psalms 119:99-100
> "I have more understanding than all my teachers, for your testimonies are my meditation. I understand more than the ancients because I keep your precepts.

CHAPTER
3

SPIRITUAL MASTERY

After saying yes to the Master to come into your heart, your next assignment is to gain an understanding of his voice and His presence. Discernment is essential to have because you will need this in every area of your life. The greatest enemy in life is ignorance. Ignorance is the major enemy of men. Add prayers and wisdom while you are at it.

God's voice is still and like calm waters. The waters may rise to their peak, but it has the potential to come to its calm at its peak. Oh, the beauty of the sea and its creatures. By design, the way you hear best from God is in the context of a friendship with Him.

Psalms 29:3-9

The voice of the Lord is upon the waters.
The God of glory thunders,
The Lord is over many waters.
The voice of the Lord is powerful,
The voice of the Lord is majestic.
The voice of the Lord breaks the cedars.
Yes, the Lord breaks in pieces the cedars
of Lebanon.

God intends for you to figure out His will freely and intelligently as you engage in regular conversations with Him. God wants to be personally present with you and having fellowship with you moment by moment as you go through life challenges. You will grow to understand Him more and become more like His Son, Jesus. For example, if someone offended you at work, your reaction is to take revenge, but you will hear a small voice telling you to retreat and to be still.

Singlehood is a time to practice hearing the voice of God, for you will encounter challenges in marriage. This is not a time to be emotionally distraught but to connect to the higher power, who is Jesus Christ, the Lamb of God.

Wisdom is a weapon and the truth. It will keep you from making mistakes in life. An educated person without wisdom is like a car without gas. Wisdom will keep you from choosing the wrong partner.

Have passionate love for God and His agenda, and He will revile Himself to you. Anything that you do with passion, it is deemed to prosper. The only way that you can survive the hardship of marriage is to seek after the Master. Your pain will be in the hand of the great I Am who will see to it that your burden becomes lighter.

Finally, my brethren, prayer is the best-kept secret. Take everything to God in prayer. Are you in distress? Do not wait for a suitable time to pray. Pray fervently in your prayer closet and never give up. The best time to pray is when the universe is sleeping at night. Get up at 3am-5am and pray. In the cool of the night, God will hear you and answer you. Communion with God is crucial. Sacrifice your time, resources and your intelligence and watch God go to work. Abraham gave the epicenter of his self-worth to God, and he was called the father of many nations.

CHAPTER
4

SINGLEHOOD HEAVEN

I did not understand the purpose of being single until I was widowed. Singlehood is a blessing in disguise, but our world does not seem to comprehend its magnitude. Are you getting to an age and you feel as though your family or friends are telling you that you are not getting any younger? That is what the naysayers will tell you to do. I am sorry to say that you are not living your life to please the Joneses or others. The decisions you make today are especially important because in the end, it will speak.

You have a lot to accomplish. This is the time to delve into knowing your purpose in life. Some of us are given God-given talents that cannot be wasted. This book was not only written for women only but for men as well. You are born with skills and talents that no one can take away from you. You must discover these talents.

Some are talented with the gift of speaking in public, and others are life coaches in the making. This will be a suitable time to have a one on one talk with God and allow the Holy Spirit to unveil who you truly are. You are not useless but useful.

Reinvent yourself by reading books and researching about your talents and you must understand that time is of the essence. Life is not waiting for you, and it is full of surprises. Enlighten yourself by going to seminars and preparing yourself for marriage if you are interested in it. Educate yourself!

Rushing into marriage without adequately preparing yourself for the journey will cost you. This is not just a warning sign to stop you in your tracks, but it is coming from an experienced sister who cares for you and wants you to succeed in your endeavors.

If you are a man, please consider researching more about the personality of a woman. God created both species, but we must understand that we are different in so many ways. The moment that this secret is revealed/disclosed to you, you have something to work with. Ladies, this is the time for you to know about the temperament of this dream man that you want to marry. Read Godly books and engage in prayer as well.

Out of desperation, single women and men are getting into marriage relationships because they are bored with themselves and feel the need that getting into a marriage will resolve their problems. Oh boy, are you wrong! It is a trap that you will regret for the rest of your life. Take your time and educate yourself in this area. The decision you make today will either break or make you. I am just keeping it real. May the Almighty God help us all.

Just like the story of the parable of the ten virgins in the bible, God has given us wisdom and understanding. Please use it for your own good!

> Mathew 25:6-10
> At midnight, the cry rang out; "Here's the bridegroom! Come out to meet him!' Then all the virgins woke up and trimmed their lamps. The foolish ones said to the wise, "Give us some of your oil; our lamps are going out. No, they replied, there may not be enough for both us and you. Instead, go

to those who sell oil and buy some for your-self.' But while they were on their way to buy the oil, the bridegroom arrived. The virgins who were ready went in with him to the wedding banquet. And the door was shut.

Everything in life takes patience and patience is a virtue. Virtues are rare in our world today. I am not only expressing myself to Christians only but to the unchurched alike. When it rains, it falls on every living creature on this planet, so I speak to the world at large. Enjoy your single-hood and make every moment count.

CHAPTER
5

EXCEPTIONAL IN EVERY WAY

Greatness does not come easy. When we look at the most talented and skilled individuals in our world today, they disciplined themselves to get to the top of the ladder. Nothing in this world worth having comes easy. According to Theodore Roosevelt- "Nothing in the world is worth having or worth doing unless it means effort, pain, difficulty... I have never in my life envied a human being who led an easy life. I have envied a great many people who led difficult lives and led them well." This statement is so true, and there is no argument about it.

There are two women in the bible that I want to discuss further. Deborah, in the book of Judges, led an exemplary life. She was a rare biblical character, a judge, a prophet, and a songwriter—a woman of many talents and yet bold like a lion. There is nothing wrong with being bold, but humility should be something to emulate.

In answering the call, Deborah became a singular biblical figure, a female leader. She recruited a man, General Barak, to stand by her side, telling him God wanted the armies of Israel to attack the Canaanites who were persecuting the highland tribes.

Deborah, in the bible, does not question God's voice or wonder what others will say or think, she simply has the faith to do what God tells her. Whether people follow or not is not her concern. Her only concern is doing what the Lord has called her to, and not letting anything get in the way of that.

Understanding the timing and seasons in your life is important. While you are preparing yourself as a single woman or man, God will prepare someone for you in your travels. When you are prepared for the battle in life, you are going to be bold and confident. That is exactly what Deborah did. She did not wait for the men in her region to say yay or nay, but she summoned the courage to go to war. Since you are equipped to be the best single person in town, you are ready for the marriage difficulties. You will know how to handle difficulties. Per chance, if you enter a marriage union, you will be able to endure and bring about change in your marriage. Let it be so!

The book of Ruth summarizes the account of this great woman. In the narrative, she is not an Israelite but came from the land of Moab and was married to an Israelite. Both her husband and her father-in-law die, and she helps her mother-in-law, Naomi, find protection. Ruth equipped herself by being useful, faithful, and hard-working after losing her husband. In her travels, she met a man who could not resist but to pay ransom to redeem this beautiful soul. Your Boaz is coming!

> Hebrew 11:6- "And without faith it is impossible to please God, because anyone who comes to him must believe that he exists and that he rewards those who earnestly seek him."

CHAPTER
6

PEACE AND PURPOSEFUL

To have peace does not come from taking a vacation because you must return to your problems after the vacation. True peace comes from the Lord. Married or not, you need the peace of God. If you are in a wrong marriage, there is no peace. I join hands with you to seek God in looking for this peace before the marriage union.

If you do not know the purpose of a thing, you will abuse it. For some of us who work in the medical field, drugs or medications are used for a purpose. If the patient does not follow the administration of the meds and begins to utilize it in an unusual way, we call that medication abuse. Everything you buy in the store has instructions or a manual on how to use that product. The manual tells you the functions of the item bought. Our manufacturer is God, and the maker of your purpose on earth asks you to come closer. Do you not know your purpose? Ask God!

As a single woman or man, begin to ask God to show you your purpose. When you know your purpose, you are at peace with God and with men. You do not have to be jealous of anyone because you know who you are. Per chance, if you do not fulfill your purpose, someone around the world will suffer. Why am I saying this? Someone may need your counsel in their marriage. Someone may need help with your educational expertise. As a single person, work on yourself; focus on changing yourself. Make up your mind to be virtuous, hardworking, patient, and wise. Prepare yourself because marriage has a purpose.

Be exceptional in every way. Are you beautiful? Use that beauty to the glory of God. Dress decently and modestly. Esther's beauty as a single woman was unfolded when the King could not sleep. She used her beauty to save a nation. Find your purpose before you get married.

The wealthiest place on this earth is in the cemetery. Millions who are dead and gone never find out their purpose; some find out their purpose, but they never fulfilled their calling. Your soul mate will find you so attractive when they see you fulfilling your God-given assignment. By the time you are ready to get married, you will be so prepared that you will manage every hardship that comes into the marriage. You will be that exceptional woman in Jesus' name.

Marriage is a complicated institution. Why am I saying this? You are going to be living with a woman or a man that you do not really know for the rest of your life, so this is important. Their mistakes will become your burden. In sickness and in health, you both must stay together and pray for each other. If there is a financial burden, you cannot run away. When there is confusion, you must endure it. Oh, what about no children? Are you going to blame your husband? May God have mercy on us and open our spiritual eyes of understanding to see the magnitude of His purpose for our lives.

A dear friend of mine prayed for me when I was going through one or two challenges in my life, and I was told to read and keep this verse of the scripture in my heart and for the rest of my life. I did not understand what the Holy Spirit was trying to tell me until now. You may have your plans all lined up, my friend, but His purpose for your life supersedes anything you are planning to do now or in the future. You must be in alignment with your God-given purpose. One can never be satisfied with the mundane things in life. God has a better plan for you, and if you follow that plan, I promise you will be happy. His purpose will always stand.

> Proverbs 19:21" There are many plans in a man's heart, nevertheless the Lord's counsel that will stand.

Chapter 7

Character Check

Some of the character traits are optimism, honesty, courage, loyalty, compassion, generosity, curiosity, kindness, confidence, empathy, self-control, imagination, and persistence. It is so difficult to talk about this subject, but it is so expedient that we discuss it. Are you working on one or two or even three of these character traits?

We must understand that no woman or man would want to marry anybody who has an ugly character. All puffed up, stack up, and conceded. You may be beautiful, but you may be using that God-created body for the wrong reasons. Do you know what a town helper means? It means you are sleeping around with every Tom, Dick, and Harry in town. It may be unlikely to find a husband.

Sorry to say that a good man sees a good woman at first or second encounter.

Some people in today's world are extremely controlling. You cannot take this to a marriage union either. It is very deadly, and if this character is not corrected, an individual may salvage relationships and stop their blessings as well.

Patience and endurance are good virtues. It is imperative to work on these two virtues as an unmarried man or woman. You will need this in everyday life. Are you going to leave a marriage if the going gets tough? This will be an enjoyable time for a Christian man or woman to seek the face of the Lord for direction and guidance.

Your husband may offend you in many ways. This is not a time to be childish and go to your mother's house for closure. Hardships such as poverty and stress will come. How do you deal with these problems, and will you have the patience to endure this trial? What about joblessness? How would you manage one person in the marriage not having a job? How would you manage this issue? When you are anointed for a purpose, you are an extremely dangerous creature. Are you willing to fail in the process of success? Praise the Lord forever more.

CHAPTER
8

CRABS IN A BARREL

When you find your purpose, you should choose your friends wisely. There is a saying that goes like this: "Show me yours friends and I will show you your future." I can briefly tell where you stand in life when I see the type of friends around you. Your friends reflect who you truly are. Let us read the book of:

Proverbs: 12-26 "The righteous should choose his friends carefully, for the way of the wicked leads them astray"

If you are around God-fearing friends, your goal in life is to please God. It is especially important that you surround yourself with purpose-driven and God-fearing friends while you are single or in a marriage. Why am I saying this? They can either derail your progress or push you to do better in life.

Some friends will come to exploit you, and God appoints some to be your destiny helpers to assist you in your pilgrimage to becoming great. This is when you must use wisdom and discernment to choose who to mingle with.

The hearts of men are desperately wicked, and the enemy of your soul can send friends to you who can pretend to be lovers, but they are not. Adding prayers will ease the process as well. God will show you your enemies and your devoted friends.

Be a friend of God, and He will not fail you. True friendliness requires persistence, dedication, and determination. If you want to be friendly, show yourself friendly. God is a father, and He cares for you more than a brother. When someone loves you unconditionally, it will become obvious to you.

When you have a purpose in life, the kind of friends you should have should align with your vision in life. You cannot just have any friend because you are lonely. Some of your friends are there to pull you down, and others are there to pull you up. Have you seen crabs in a barrel? When one crab is crawling ahead, the other will be pulling down. A good friend is hard to find, but do not let him or her go when you find one. Arise, oh, sleeping giant!

CHAPTER
9

THE PURPOSE OF A MAN

The purpose of a man is to know God, lead, and be responsible. In the book of Genesis, the man was created first and was put in Eden to work and secondly to be in His presence. God made a man to work, cultivate, protect, and obey his word. Pursue God first and his presence. The key to manhood is work. The first commandment God gave man was to work and secondly to be in his presence.

Work means to become, fulfill, manifest, reveal, to become yourself. Your work is your purpose and a gift. God is saying to become. God has hidden in a man an awesome plan to become great. The job you are doing is only temporary. With that said, manifest who you really are. Manifest your talents and your skills. You cannot fire a gift.

You cannot fire Michael Jordan, Lebron James, or Tiger Woods because they are gifted. Their gifts are permanent.

Vision is purpose in pictures. Your worth is your work. When you do not work, you feel like you are useless. Your work is your vision. If you find your purpose and see it in pictures, you are on the right path to success.

> Proverbs 19:21
> Many are the plans in a man's heart, but it is
> the Lord's purpose that prevails."

After finding your purpose, which is your work, God will present the woman that you are looking for. Without work, my advice to men around the world is not to even think of marriage. A man without work is a disaster about to happen. That is the reason a man becomes frustrated and blames his wife for everything.

My friend, God has given women wisdom, intellect, and intelligence and all these skills are to assist you with your vision. Some men are intimidated when they see an intelligent woman. Why! If a man has a vision or goal, he should never be intimidated by an intelligent woman. A great woman is a blessing in disguise.

Chapter 10

The Purpose of a Woman

The quality of a good woman is rare. A God-fearing woman is ridiculously hard to find, so that is why you must seek after her like rubies. A good woman is not lazy but productive. A good and intelligent woman goes the extra mile and works hard to support his husband and the home. A good woman has a heart of giving.

Proverbs 31:25 starts out by saying, "she is clothed with strength and dignity...." The word dignity has been defined as the state or quality of being worthy of honor or respect. Not only are you covered in strength, but you are also worthy of honor and respect as well.

After God told Adam to work in Eden, he gave him a helper. The helper was Eve. Your helper (woman) is to help you, so if a man is not working, how can she help you. The woman becomes frustrated if there is no project to work on. A woman is equipped to help a man's vision.

A WOMAN IS TO COMPLETE A MAN. This is a revelation. A woman is frustrated when a man is not working. What were you born to do? Man of God, find out your vision now before you find that wife. Your wife needs security, not frustration.

If a woman finds out there is no vision for her to follow, you will find out many of these women will venture into their own businesses and take over the pulpits. In the book of Judges, when all the men did not want to go to war, Deborah stood up and swore to herself to lead.

A good woman is wise in counsel. A good woman should be an asset, not a burden. Take diligent care of yourself and dress modestly for your husband. Everything you touch should multiply, and your husband will call you blessed.

Finally, I will preach to the entire world that a woman who fears the Lord is the most beautiful being in this world. To fear the Lord is to do His will. My fellow sisters in the Lord, you were created for a purpose, and now that you know what you are supposed to do, you will not take your husband or aspiring husband's glory. You are to help your future husband, and he will praise you at the gates. Just like Proverbs 31 summarized.

Chapter
11

MARRIAGE IS A COMMITMENT, NOT LOVE

Indeed, marriage is not being in love, but it is all about commitment. Marriage is a covenant between two individuals who are willing to commit to each other through sickness and in health. This union is not for young and immature boys and girls. It requires sacrifice and patience and the ability to let go of your pride and prejudices.

I will advise that before you get into this union, you read about my advice on singlehood again in chapters 1 and 3 of this book before you make any type of decision. Marriage can be a blessing, or it can be a thorn in your flesh if you know what I mean.

If you find someone who loves the Lord, cares, and genuinely appreciates you, you are on your way to greatness. The plan of God is for that marriage to prosper so the family can be of service to the rest of the world.

The idea of marriage was not constituted when God created Adam and Eve, but it already existed in His kingdom. The church is His bride, and God is so jealous of His creation. We were made in the image of God, and He wants us to connect with Him daily so we can receive grace in times of need.

If you genuinely had prayed to God that you need a partner, He will lead you to the right person, but one thing that He will not do is to choose for you. One thing that you must know about God is that He is a perfect gentleman and is supreme as well. He will not impose; neither will He decide for you. God can present an individual to you, but it is up to you to pray and seek guidance from the Almighty Creator. He can even go further by showing you dreams and visions of this individual. Again, it is up to you to make that weighty decision.

You must understand that God created Adam and presented Eve to him. Adam could have said no to God. When things heated up in the Garden of Eden, Adam blamed God for giving him a helpmate. It is just like salvation. You must decide to accept or reject God as your personal savior. It is the same with evangelism, you can tell people about Christ, but you cannot force them to know Him. The Holy Spirit will do the prompting. At this point, the choice is yours to make.

Please do not mistake sensual feelings for love. When that feeling fades away in the marriage, what else is left? Before marriage, it is important to make sure there is a bond. What do I mean? Can both of you understand each other? Can both come to terms with an issue? Can a problem in the marriage be resolved immediately when it arises? Are both able to compromise? Marriage is a serious business, my friend.

Having children is another issue that we need to discuss. You need to know that children are a blessing, but they are also an add-on to the family. The training and the wellbeing of your children is another challenge. I do not want to discourage you from getting married, but I want you to weigh the cost. If you are not spiritually sound, mature, and prepared for this challenge, it will take you by surprise. Awake, children of God!

My friend, you must deal with family members as well. Sometimes, you may have a challenge with one or two family members. As a mature and spiritual Christian, how do you handle it? Some will leave their marriage because of family members. They are part of your family. Are you going to ignore them or deal with them according to the love of Christ?

Church differences can be an obstacle in a marriage. We are serving a mighty God. Apart from Jesus, I do not know any other name under the heavens. It is beautiful for a couple to go to one church, but how do couples handle these church differences? If the church is serving this Jesus and walking in His steps, then there is nothing wrong with visiting another church, but there should be understanding. Some churches are not serving God but in for other things, but church differences can bring a challenge in marriage. Stay in His presence.

Take care of yourself when you are in a relationship. The Proverbs thirty-one verse is detailed and informative. In Proverbs 31: 22-23, it reads, she makes tapestry for herself; her clothing is fine linen and purple. Her husband is known in the gates." There is something irresistible about a woman who takes care of herself. Just because you have four children does not mean you have to look like you have been hit by a train. Dress modestly and groom yourself for your men. Likewise, for our man, you must look good for your spouse.

Another asset is to keep yourself busy as a woman. There are some of the things that a woman can do to improve the household. In Proverbs 31, this woman is hardworking and sells at the marketplace as well. God forbid something happens to the family. I pray that you will not be looking around for assistance. For the help of men is vain. Start educating yourself. Think big and be creative. Please read on.

> Proverbs 31:24-27" She makes linen garments and sells them and supplies sashes for the merchants. Strength and honor are her clothing; She shall rejoice in time to come. She opens her mouth with wisdom, and on her tongue is the law of kindness. She watches over the ways of her household and does not eat the bread of idleness."

CHAPTER
12

COMMUNICATION

Communication is between two people. One can be listening, and the other do the talking. It is important that when you are dealing with the Holy God, communion becomes a key factor to your success. I am telling you, friends, that if you work diligently on the way you communicate with God and men, you are on your way to greatness. You must make a way for the Holy Spirit to speak to you after praying.

We are on earth to support each other, and when you work hard to achieve this goal, blessed are you! The way you carry yourself and deal with your friends and acquaintances surely can champion you into your destiny. Who wants to talk to a nasty man or woman? Respect goes a long way.

Sometimes you do not have to agree with that person you are communicating with, but you can give that individual respect and dignity. Yelling and talking over another individual is not communicating.

Active listening is part of communication. God can change your destiny and your situation if you can only listen. Sometimes, God can use your friends, billboards, bumper stickers or a sign to direct or guide you to your desired outcome. Your blessings are in your listening. Those business ideas that you have been praying about is in your listening.

This book came about at the midnight hour when I woke up from my sleep. As I was praying, the Holy Spirit guided me to start listening to my favorite preacher at around 3:15 am, and I captured the title of my second book. We are poor because we are still doing the "same old."

For this individual that you want to get married to, do you understand each other? While communicating with each other daily, there should be an understanding, taking turns to speak and respecting each other. When you respect someone, your mannerism during a brief conversation is crucial to the growth of that relationship.

Understanding is the willingness to show kind or favorable feelings towards others. It is also an agreement of opinion or feeling. This person that you want to marry must understand you in some way. Yes, sometimes you may agree to disagree, but that does not mean that both cannot come into an agreement. Please understand that if you come together as a couple, you may have to come together to decide on an important matter, and it will be very selfish of both parties to make a foolish decision. Be wise as a serpent. A serpent does not make a lot of noise when it is about to bite. It is a smooth operator. It will bite when you are not looking.

Understanding is knowledge and power. Understanding is a weapon. There is a realm of power and influence in understanding. You are born for something better. Understanding will bring you before kings and queens. Shalom, my brothers and sisters.

CHAPTER
13

SACRIFICE YOUR LAMB

In Christianity, the lamb represents Christ as both suffering and triumphant; It is typically a sacrificial animal and may also symbolize gentleness, innocence, and purity. In addition, the lamb symbolizes sweetness, forgiveness, and meekness.

Abraham, by faith, was about to sacrifice his only son, but it was that his faith could be tested. Why was Abraham inspired to do the will of God? This was a testament of endurance. Sacrifice can teach an individual discipline and patience; where death ends is where resurrection starts.

Marriage is indeed sacrificial. You must understand that when two people get married, there is a spiritual dimension to this union. It is not always going to be your way but the way of the Lord. Your selfish desires should be relegated to the background. In order to accept the best, let the power of the Holy Spirit transform your mindset.

Forgiveness is something that you do every day in your marriage. Some are enduring marriage because they refuse to let go of the past. Forgiveness can heal your marriage and salvage the many years of dishonesty. No matter what the problem is, please bury it and let it go. Has he or she defamed your character? The only way to let go is to give it to the Master. The Lord alone can give you the grace to forgive your partner.

Meekness is not being a doormat in a marriage. It is best to save your marriage than to argue every day and end up in a divorce. Being humble allows the other partner in the relationship to see things in a different dimension. It is challenging to give in and to be the one to bring peace, but it will pay off.

My fellow brothers and sisters, in life, you must give in to others to receive. When your life is about giving, then you are truly ready to receive. Do not always be in the position to receive. When you are self-centered, it is hard for you to receive. In your singlehood or in your marriage, practice doing good and watch what God will do in your life. If you want a breakthrough, pour into other people's life, and this will bring you into your new season. You can be right some of the time but when conflicts arise, be the one to bring peace and tranquility into the relationship.

> Genesis 18: 6-10 "And Abraham hurried into the tent to Sarah and said, "Quickly, make ready three measures of fine meal; knead it and make cakes." And Abraham ran to the herd, took a tender and good calf, gave it to a young man, and he hastened to prepare it. So, he took butter and milk and the calf which he had prepared and set it before them; and he stood by them under the tree as they ate. Then thy said to him, "Where is Sarah your wife?' So, he said. Here, in the tent. And He said, "I will certainly return to you according to the time of life, and behold, Sarah, your wife shall have a son." (Sarah was listening in the tent door which was behind him.)

Chapter
14

Your Pain is Your Glory

I ndeed, your pain is your glory. If you can do your research, those sitting in high places today did not come easily before their lifting. Pain is described as physical suffering. Physical suffering can cause mental, psychological, and emotional pain. Pain is the number one cause of suicidal ideations and depression. Some are on long-term medications because of the effects of pain.

Some are in the wrong relationships because of pain. They are running from one person to the other, seeking refuge, but your deliverance is not in these relationships. Stop and rewind! Pain can be a good thing if you know where the source is from.

Once you know the source of that pain, one can bring their cares to the Almighty God. The Almighty God created you and understood the root cause of this hurt or pain. He can change your situation and turn it into gold. Before we can get refined gold, it undergoes harsh treatment. If you do not experience these challenges, how are you going to shine?

What experiences do you have so you can coach and counsel others? Unless you have been in the same predicament before, you have no right to educate someone about a particular problem. God allows pain in our life for a purpose. God is sitting high and looking low at your situation, and He knows your beginning from the end.

Your ministry or your purpose might require that you go through this painful experience to further minister to souls around the world. When pain is ongoing, surrender your cares and burdens to the Lord, and he will give you the peace that surpasses all understanding. It is not easy to do just that, but the answer is in your obedience to the Lord.

Abraham waited for the promise and had a son. Moses left Egypt and pilgrimage to a land unknown. The riches that he had once known was not accessible. He humbled himself to be equipped and nurtured by God, and when his time came, he was able to deliver the people of Israel to their desired location.

Do not ever question God when you are going through tough times. Could it be that you are the Moses that God is looking for? Could it be that you are the David that God is seeking after? If God wants to use you mightily, look at your trials and tribulations in your life. Now, let us talk about your glory.

God's glory upon your life will come when you have passed the test of time. One thing I have noticed is when someone is anointed for a purpose, it does not come easily. That individual is disciplined, calm, cool and collected, spiritually mature, wise and lives a genuine righteous life. The glory of God will come upon that individual when he/she speaks. Their speech makes a difference. They are humble, not pompous.

If you are going through financial and marital problems, you are being prepared for a ministry beyond you. Your ministry is in that pain. You might be a financier to the kingdom of God. That is why you are having these financial problems. Sell your pain to the world.

Do not be bitter when you are going through the challenges of life. It will be bittersweet to see the end results. Your glory is great. Your future is rest assured. The Holy Spirit will lead you to own the pond. There is a difference between someone teaching you how to fish than owning the pond. If I teach you how to fish, perchance the owner of that pond might send you away because you are taking all the fish in the pond, but if I teach you how to own that pond, you will be a source of comfort and help to those who are struggling financially. Shalom, my brothers and sisters.

CHAPTER
15

ABIGAIL, THE
OPPORTUNITY BROKER

You are a package send to earth by God to be a carrier of God's purpose. A gift is an inherited capacity which was put in human beings to perform a function. Everything in creation was created with a gift. Your gift is the source of your value. Your value comes from your gift. God created everything with a gift.

You are born to deliver something the world needs. Your gift is your source of value. Your purpose produces the gift. A seed is carrying a gift. The gift of the tree is its fruits. Your gifts are to help others. The gift of the leaves of a tree has oxygen. Nothing in life is useless. If your gift is valuable, people will maintain you. You are indeed a gift to the world.

The gift of the bird is flight. The gift of a fish is the capacity to swim. Whatever your gift is, you came with it when you were born. The sun is a gift. Jesus Christ came to the world to be a gift, and if you do not connect with this gift, your purpose can never be fulfilled.

When God created you, he placed a gift inside you. Your children carry a seed, and you may never know what gift and talents God has placed in them. You are pregnant with a gift. You are born to solve a problem. If you love yourself, keep investing in yourself.

How do you know if you have a gift? You will know it when you have many setbacks with an issue or when you complain about something repeatedly. For example, if you are poor or having marital problems, God is telling you that is where you will succeed. For the person who is poor, God wants you to start thinking out of the box and to be creative. If there is no Goliath, there will not be a David. If you want to be great, look for a problem to resolve. You might be the one to create jobs for others.

For the individual going through marital problems, you may be the one God will use to deliver or help people with marital issues. Just remember that your gift is not for you to keep, but it is for others to enjoy. It is the price you must pay that will earn you the right to be influential or respected.

You must put a seed in the dirt for it to germinate. Yes, in order to achieve your purpose, people will put dirt on you. In other words, people will disrespect, gossip, and defame your character, but hold on. If you still hold on to that vision, nobody can stop you.

If you are redefining yourself when the time comes to get married, you will not be intimidated by an intelligent woman or a goal-driven or visionary man. When two people come together as a couple, and they understand each other, it is like an atomic bomb. Everything that they put their hands to do will prosper because they understand the power of purpose. They are not afraid to support each other. They are not afraid to correct each other in love.

Let us look at the story of Abigail and Nabal in 1 Samuel. Abigail was an intelligent and beautiful woman. In contrast, Nabal was mean in his dealings. When David sent his men to Nabal to deliver a particularly important message, Nabal acted foolishly and ended up dying in the process; however, his wife used her God-given talents;

her calm response, wisdom, understanding, and beauty to calm down the angry King David.

> I Samuel 25 :18-19
> Abigail acted quickly. She took two hundred loaves of bread, two skins of wine, five dressed sheep, five seahs of roasted grain, a hundred cakes of raisins and two hundred cakes of pressed figs and loaded them on donkeys. Then she told her servants, "Go on ahead; I will follow you. But she did not tell her husband, Nabal.

You can be connected to your purpose if you are humbled to know who God is sending your way. Abigail was a wise lady and understood her purpose. She resolved a problem and was a helper indeed. This is the kind of woman that a man is looking for. Her husband acted foolishly, but she did not. Please read on:

> I Samuel 25: 23-25
> When Abigail saw David, she quickly got off her donkey and bowed down before David

with her to the ground. She fell at his feet
and said: "Pardon your servant, my lord,
and let me speak to you; hear what your servant has to say. Please pay no attention, my
lord, to that wicked man Nabal. He is just
like his name-his name means fool, and folly
goes with him, and as for me, your servant, I
did not see the men my Lord sent.

In summary, marriage is to be enjoyed, not to be
endured. It is a God-ordained office that many cannot
fulfill. Marriage is sacrificial and demands persistence
and endurance. Marriage is not love but a covenant that
cannot be broken. One cannot go in and out as they
pleased. While you are in the marriage, you must find a
way to respect the other person. Do not get into a marriage if you are not prepared spiritually, mentally, emotionally, and psychologically. It will take a toll on you if
you are not ready to deal with life's difficulties.

Seasons will change, and people will change. Are you
ready to accept the changing seasons? Are you ready to
bear the shame, pain, and inconsistencies? Take time and
take it to the Lord in prayer when you are making this

historic decision. This decision can be a life-changer or a life breaker. Marriage can uplift, and it can also put you in chains. It will be a disaster to see you in chains. I want to see you happy and enjoy every part of your life with your spouse and children.

Take your cares and your burdens to God in prayers. Submit your request to the Almighty God, who knows what is best for you. There is someone that God has prepared for you, and you will not miss this person if you are in constant communication with the Creator. HE will send you your Boaz or Ruth at the right time, and you will enjoy the fruit of your labor together.

For the marriage that is in shambles or total disorder, I pray that you will find rest in the everlasting arms of God. There is nothing that He cannot fix. Every tear is recorded in His book, and He will never disappoint you. Your pain will be your glory at the end.

CHAPTER
16

HOLY SPIRIT & PRAYER

We discussed earlier that God will never choose a partner for you. HE can assist you in choosing this partner. Love does not keep marriage together. A successful marriage is a result of the application of knowledge, not the exchange of love. Love is just pure emotions; Love is a choice. Emotions can change at any time; just remember that. You also have the Holy Spirit, common sense, discernment, spiritual leaders, Godly friends, and parents to guide you when making this historic decision.

God is love, and He has placed a value on you. Agape love is unconditional love. Jesus loved those who hated him and died on the cross so we can be saved. I cannot die on the cross for you, and neither can your spouse sacrifice

Your Pain is Your Glory

his or her life for you. Human beings do not understand true love. Human beings abuse the concept of love. Do not get married because of love. It is a trick.

Your spouse should intimately have a divine intimate relationship with the Holy Spirit, and yet it is still not even enough to say yes," I will marry you." A man that can care for you when you mess up or when there is no child, my dear, is operating in agape love. Any condition becomes an expectation because nothing in life remains the same. After the fifth child, you are not going to be looking the same. Can he still love you? Ladies, you use to be "figure 8," but now, you are not. Can he look past that? It takes a Godly man to look beyond this beauty and see the beauty that God has created in you. What if your spouse loses his job and you must move from your beautiful house back to an apartment? Ladies, are you able to endure, or are you going to lash out at this man? What if both of you lose your jobs? Are you willing to stay in the marriage? Marriage is an application of knowledge. Use wisdom, and wisdom is God.

Oh, the presence of the Holy Spirit can do you good. You need His presence to strive currently and in your marriage. The Holy Spirit is a guide and a comforting friend.

The Holy Spirit is God, and He represents the eternal presence of Jesus. The Holy Spirit is the wisdom of God, the reviler, and the author of the word of God. The person of the Holy Spirit is a mystery. There is no reason for you to doubt His presence. Married couples, when you are worn out, call on the Holy Spirit. The Holy Spirit is gentle, so He will not impose on you. He has more knowledge than all the professors in this world combined.

> John 16:14" However, when He, the Spirit of truth, has come, He will guide you into all truth: for He will not speak on His own authority, but whatever He will tell you things to come. He will glorify me, for He will take of what is mine and declare it to you."

His presence is soothing, and He will show you all things. I have encountered His love during the challenges of life. His presence will equip you for your purpose. He teaches you the word of God and sanctifies (set apart for a particular use) you. HE empowers us as well. Your marriage is to bring glory to God, and he is there to help you each step of the way. He helps you with your weaknesses as well. Martin Luther King Jr., quoted that "Nothing in all the world is more dangerous than sincere ignorance and conscientious stupidity." Ignorance of His presence will cost you as a Christian.

Be a person of consistent prayer. Take marriage as a spiritual union, and you should always be praying. The Holy Spirit will unfold things to you ahead of time, so you will not be surprised by what comes your way. There are times when things are not always rosy in marriage. Prayer will keep you from filing for a divorce. It will help you to operate under open heavens, ask for divine helpers and command your day. Stay in His secret place, and you will have rest for your soul. Please read this chapter of the bible about this great woman of God:

> Luke 2:36-38 "Now there was one, Anna, a prophetess, the daughter of Phanuel of the tribe of Asher, She was of a great age, and had lived with a husband seven years from her virginity; and this woman was a widow of about eighty-four years, who did not depart from the temple, but served God

with fasting and prayers night and day and coming in that instant she gave thanks to the Lord, and spoke to Him to all those who looked for redemption in Jerusalem.

Prayer:

Holy Spirit, I pray for your power and presence over all the marriages and the single people around the world today. Show us your glory and empower us to do more than we can do. May your presence be known to all men and show us the mind of God for our lives, Amen!

CHAPTER 17

COUNSELING FOR SINGLEHOOD AND MARRIAGE

My goal or aim is for you to understand that you are not alone with this important decision-making in your lifetime, and my recommendation is to reach out to the Holy Spirit first and a spiritually God-fearing trusted friend. Joint effort with this individual in prayer before you make any unwise decisions. Just like Rebecca met Isaac, may the Spirit of God connect you to your partner. For those who are going through marital challenges, your source of help is the Holy Spirit. Keep your eyes on the cross, and remember that there is no pain without gain— my love to the families around the world.

For the widows and widowers around the world, God is your helper and a constant friend. HE will be your strength when you are weak. Never live without His presence. Rest assured that you are not alone. The grieving process is not easy, but I personally have been there before. The Holy Spirit can do more for you than a family member. Cheer up and keep your eyes on the cross. The challenges you are experiencing today is your ministry, and it is for His glory to be revealed. Learn how to fellowship with the Holy Spirit.

For those who are not born-again or unchurched, please pray with me:

> Father, I ask for mercy on behalf of those who are lost. Let your mercy fill their hearts that they may be able to know that you are the true living God who was and is to come. Help them know that it is only in surrendering themselves to you that they will find real rest and unconditional love. The Holy Spirit is the key to your salvation. Amen!

Additional Resources

- Author's Personal email:
  Yvonnekubi5@gmail.com
- Life Coach/ Marriage Consultation/Business/
  Educational Ideas/Case Management:
  Yvonnekubi5@gmail.com
- Marital Resources: Family Life Radio at :https://
  www.myflr.org
- Radio Station/Church: Zoelight Gospel Radio:
  www.zoelightradio.com or www.zenithchapel.org
- Home Health Services in Maryland: https://
  hphomecareservices.com
- Social Services Organization in Columbia,
  Maryland (FIRN): www.beluminus.org
- Adult Grief Support: www.caringmatters.org
- Non-profit Organization (Community Action
  Council of Howard County): www.cac-hc.org

Additional Reading

MEDITATION

Psalms 107:30-31

Then they are glad because they are quite; so, He guides them to their desired haven. Oh, that men would give thanks to the Lord for His goodness, and for His wonderful works to the children of men!

Order Books Online

Please order my books on Amazon, Target, Wallmart, Apple books, Barnes and Nobles, Books a million and Xulon Press website.

- ➤ Your Current Location is Not Your final Destination in the Process-Yvonne Kubi
- ➤ Your Pain is Your Glory; Singlehood to Marital Bliss-Yvonne Kubi
- ➤ Children's Books- Coming soon

CPSIA information can be obtained
at www.ICGtesting.com
Printed in the USA
LVHW052004191021
700869LV00013B/419